you, me
and the
Bible

A reading guide to the six central ideas of the Bible

**based on
Two Ways to Live**

Tony Payne

SYDNEY · YOUNGSTOWN

Matthias Media
(St Matthias Press Ltd ACN 067 558 365)
Email: info@matthiasmedia.com.au
Internet: www.matthiasmedia.com.au
Please visit our website for current postal and telephone contact information.

Matthias Media (USA)
Email: sales@matthiasmedia.com
Internet: www.matthiasmedia.com
Please visit our website for current postal and telephone contact information.

ISBN 978 1 922206 57 2

Cover design and typesetting by Matthias Media.

CONTENTS

Introduction

It's strange how we often form strong opinions about things we actually don't know very much about—whether about politics or sport, or about whether that famous person on trial at the moment is really guilty or not.

The teaching of the Bible falls into this category for many people. We know it as a big black book that Christians look to as the source of their beliefs. But it's amazing how many of us have never actually read it for ourselves.

That's the aim of *You, Me and the Bible*. It provides an opportunity for friends to sit down together and see what the Bible really says about God, and the world, and life and death, and what our lives are about.

Over the next six sessions, you'll do this by reading a number of key passages from the Bible and discussing them together. The passages we've selected cover six of the most foundational ideas and events of the Bible, and provide a good overview of its central message.

Each session contains two short Bible passages in a modern English translation, along with some discussion questions to kick off the conversation. Please use these questions as a guide and help to talk about what the passage means, not as a rigid set of tasks you must complete.

Questions like this will get you talking about the actual content of the passage. Try these first, straight after you read the passage.

Questions like this will help you think further about what the passage means for us and for our world.

After reading the two passages in each session, there is also a summary of the main ideas for you to discuss.

Some basic Bible facts to get you started:

- The Bible presents itself as the record of God's personal revelation to the world—starting with his creation of the world and finishing with a vision of how God's plans for the world and humanity will finally be fulfilled at the end of time.

- The Bible is one long story, but is composed of 66 separate books written between approximately 1300BC and 80AD.

- These books are divided into the 'Old Testament' and the 'New Testament'.

old testament   new testament

- The Old Testament is made up of 39 books written between approximately 1300BC and 450BC, and largely focuses on God's dealings with the nation of Israel and his promises for the future of the world.

- The New Testament comprises 27 books written between approximately 50AD and 80AD, and is mainly about Jesus Christ and his fulfilment of God's promises in the Old Testament.

- There are many different kinds of writing in the collection of books that makes up the Bible: history, poetry, biography, letters, prophecy, and so on.

- In *You, Me and the Bible*, you will be looking at a number of these different types of writing, ranging from Genesis (the first book of the Bible) all the way through to Revelation (the last book).

- For the convenience of being able to refer easily to particular sections, the individual books of the Bible are divided into chapters and verses. So 'Genesis 12:14-16' means the book of Genesis, chapter 12, verses 14 to 16.

For a brief video introduction to You, *Me and the Bible*, go to matthiasmedia.com/ymb/introvid.

PASSAGE 1

Genesis 1:26-28, 31

Genesis is the first book of the Bible. This passage is part of the account of God's creation of the world. In the verses just before our passage, God has created the world, the land, the seas, the sun and stars, and the plants and animals.

old testament

new testament

1

What do we learn about humanity in this passage?

2

What responsibility does God give to mankind?

3

What does God think of all that he has made?

Then God said, "Let us make mankind in our image, in our likeness, so that they may rule over the fish in the sea and the birds in the sky, over the livestock and all the wild animals, and over all the creatures that move along the ground".

> So God created mankind in his own image, in the image of God he created them; male and female he created them.

God blessed them and said to them, "Be fruitful and increase in number; fill the earth and subdue it. Rule over the fish in the sea and the birds in the sky and over every living creature that moves on the ground"...

God saw all that he had made, and it was very good. And there was evening, and there was morning—the sixth day.

What picture of God do we get in this passage?

Do you see the world as "very good"? Why/why not?

What do you think might be the implications of us being made 'in God's image'?

If humanity is supposed to be 'in charge' of the world (under God), what sort of job are we doing, do you think?

7

PASSAGE 2

Revelation 4:6-11

We now move from the first to the very last book of the Bible. Revelation is a bit like a dream sequence in a movie—where the author (the apostle John) is shown a vision of what is taking place in heaven, and of what the future holds. Many passages in the book of Revelation are full of rich imagery and symbolism, including this passage from chapter 4. It features a picture of all of creation (represented by four symbolic 'living creatures') and the leaders of God's people (the '24 elders') assembled around God's throne.

old testament   new testament

In the centre, around the throne, were four living creatures, and they were covered with eyes, in front and in back. The first living creature was like a lion, the second was like an ox, the third had a face like a man, the fourth was like a flying eagle. Each of the four living creatures had six wings and was covered with eyes all around, even under its wings. Day and night they never stop saying:

> *"'Holy, holy, holy**
> *is the Lord God Almighty',*
> *who was, and is, and is to come."*

Whenever the living creatures give glory, honour and thanks to him who sits on the throne and who lives for ever and ever, the twenty-four elders fall down before him who sits on the throne and worship him who lives for ever and ever. They lay their crowns before the throne and say:

> *"You are worthy, our Lord and God,*
> *   to receive glory and honour and power,*
> *for you created all things,*
> *   and by your will they were created*
> *   and have their being."*

1

What sort of God is described here?

2

What responses do you see in the passage to this God?

3

What does the creation owe to its creator?

The Bible presents God both creator of all an ruler over all. What's t connection between the two ideas, do you think

Do you believe that a king or ruler can be truly good?

What does God need from us?

* 'Holy' means 'distinct' or 'set apart'—in this case referring to how unique and completely different from us God is.

8

Pulling it together

How would you use the following diagram to summarize the key ideas of the two passages we've read?

For a brief video summary, go to matthiasmedia.com/ymb/vid1.

What's your own reaction to the idea of God being the creator and ruler of the world?

Do you ever think of yourself as a 'creature' (that is, as having been created by Someone)? How do you feel about this?

How do these passages compare with your experience of the world?

Want to read more?
Acts 17:24-25
1 Corinthians 8:5-6
Colossians 1:15-20

PASSAGE 1

Genesis 3:1-6

This passage picks up the story after the creation of the man (Adam) and woman (Eve) by God. They have been placed in a beautiful garden where they have all that they need.

old testament   new testament

1 How would you describe the serpent's strategy for persuading the woman to eat the fruit?

2 What does the fruit symbolize, do you think?

3 What does Eve (and Adam) hope to gain?

Now the serpent was more crafty than any of the wild animals the LORD God had made. He said to the woman, "Did God really say, 'You must not eat from any tree in the garden'?"

The woman said to the serpent, "We may eat fruit from the trees in the garden, but God did say, 'You must not eat fruit from the tree that is in the middle of the garden, and you must not touch it, or you will die'".

"You will not certainly die", the serpent said to the woman. "For God knows that when you eat from it your eyes will be opened, and you will be like God, knowing good and evil."

When the woman saw that the fruit of the tree was good for food and pleasing to the eye, and also desirable for gaining wisdom, she took some and ate it. She also gave some to her husband, who was with her, and he ate it.

How would you summarize humanity's attitude towards God in this passage?

Do you perceive this attitude towards God in your own life and heart? If so, how does it come out?

11

PASSAGE 2

Romans 1:18-25

This passage is from one of the most well-known letters in the New Testament, written by the apostle Paul to the Christians in Rome.

old testament

new testament

1 What can all people everywhere know about God?

2 On what basis can they know this?

3 What do people do instead?

4 What are the consequences?

The wrath* of God is being revealed from heaven against all the godlessness and wickedness of people, who suppress the truth by their wickedness, since what may be known about God is plain to them, because God has made it plain to them. For since the creation of the world God's invisible qualities—his eternal power and divine nature—have been clearly seen, being understood from what has been made, so that people are without excuse.

For although they knew God, they neither glorified him as God nor gave thanks to him, but their thinking became futile and their foolish hearts were darkened. Although they claimed to be wise, they became fools and exchanged the glory of the immortal God for images† made to look like a mortal human being and birds and animals and reptiles.

Therefore God gave them over in the sinful desires of their hearts to sexual impurity for the degrading of their bodies with one another. They exchanged the truth about God for a lie, and worshipped and served created things rather than the Creator—who is forever praised. Amen.

Do you notice any similarities between this passage and the one from Genesis 3 (about Adam and Eve and the serpent)?

Can you think of ways in which people today worship and serve "created things rather than the Creator"?

Do you think it's possible to be quite religious and yet still to be rebelling against God our creator?

★ 'Wrath' means 'anger'.
+ The 'images' Paul talks about are statues or idols used in pagan worship.

Pulling it together

*How would you use the following diagram to summarize
the key ideas of the two passages we've read?*

For a brief video summary, go to matthiasmedia.com/ymb/vid2.

What do you think is
the root cause of the
suffering and injustice
in our world?

Do you see yourself in either
of these passages? How
would you describe your own
relationship with God (the
creator and ruler)?

What do you think
God should do about
humanity's rebellion
against him?

Want to read more?

Proverbs 20:9
Romans 3:9-20
Galatians 5:19-21

Part 3

PASSAGE 1

Deuteronomy 29:16-20

After the fall of Adam and Eve, God chose a particular man (Abraham) and the nation that came from him (Israel) to be the focus of his plans for the world. In this passage, the people of Israel have been rescued from slavery in Egypt, and Moses (their leader at the time) is addressing them as they prepare to enter the Promised Land.

1 What attitudes and actions is Moses warning against?

2 What will be the consequences for those who don't heed the warning?

old testament   new testament

You yourselves know how we lived in Egypt and how we passed through the countries on the way here. You saw among them their detestable images and idols of wood and stone, of silver and gold. Make sure there is no man or woman, clan or tribe among you today whose heart turns away from the LORD* our God to go and worship the gods of those nations; make sure there is no root among you that produces such bitter poison.

When such a person hears the words of this oath+ and they invoke a blessing on themselves, thinking, "I will be safe, even though I persist in going my own way", they will bring disaster on the watered land as well as the dry. The LORD will never be willing to forgive them; his wrath‡ and zeal will burn against them. All the curses written in this book will fall on them, and the LORD will blot out their names from under heaven.

Do you think it is just and reasonable that God should punish people for rebelling against him?

Anger and zeal are not always good things in our experience. But here God is described as getting angry and zealous. What's going on, do you think?

How do you think the anger of God might relate to the love of God?

---

* 'LORD' (in small capitals) is a reference to the personal name of God, which in Hebrew is represented by the letters YHWH.

+ 'This oath' refers to the covenant or agreement that God is making with Israel—for his part to be their God and to take them to the Promised Land, and for their part to keep his laws and be faithful to him.

‡ 'Wrath' means 'anger'.

15

PASSAGE 2

2 Thessalonians 1:6-10

This passage is from Paul's second letter to the Christians in Thessalonica, who (like many in our world today) were being persecuted and mistreated for being Christians.

old testament new testament

> *God is just: He will pay back trouble to those who trouble you and give relief to you who are troubled, and to us as well. This will happen when the Lord Jesus is revealed from heaven in blazing fire with his powerful angels. He will punish those who do not know God and do not obey the gospel of our Lord Jesus. They will be punished with everlasting destruction and shut out from the presence of the Lord and from the glory of his might on the day he comes to be glorified in his holy people and to be marvelled at among all those who have believed. This includes you, because you believed our testimony to you.*

1

Who will be punished by whom?

2

Why will they be punished?

3

When will this happen?

4

What is the punishment?

In this passage it's the 'Lord Jesus' who comes bringing punishment on those who oppose him. How does this square with your picture of who Jesus is?

"People today have a love-hate relationship with the idea of judgement."
Do you think that's right?
Why/why not?

16

Pulling it together

*How would you use the following diagram to summarize
the key ideas of the two passages we've read?*

For a brief video summary, go to matthiasmedia.com/ymb/vid3.

Given all that we've seen so far, what sort of problem does humanity face?

What's your own reaction to the Bible's message about God's anger and judgement against those who rebel against him?

Want to read more?
Psalm 98:9
Ecclesiastes 12:14
Matthew 12:36
Luke 12:5

PASSAGE 1

Isaiah 53:3-6, 9-10

The Old Testament tells the story of Israel being chosen and blessed by God, but then constantly rebelling against him and suffering the consequences. Some 800 years before the time of Jesus, the prophet Isaiah wrote about a 'servant' whom God would one day send to rescue people from their rebellion against him.

old testament

new testament

He was despised and rejected by mankind,
a man of suffering, and familiar with pain.
Like one from whom people hide their faces
he was despised, and we held him in low esteem.

Surely he took up our pain
and bore our suffering,
yet we considered him punished by God,
stricken by him, and afflicted.
But he was pierced for our transgressions, *
he was crushed for our iniquities;
the punishment that brought us peace was on him,
and by his wounds we are healed.
We all, like sheep, have gone astray,
each of us has turned to our own way;
and the LORD has laid on him
the iniquity+ of us all...

He was assigned a grave with the wicked,
and with the rich in his death,
though he had done no violence,
nor was any deceit in his mouth.

Yet it was the LORD's will to crush him and cause him to suffer,
and though the LORD makes his life an offering for sin,
he will see his offspring and prolong his days,
and the will of the LORD will prosper in his hand.

1

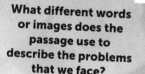

What different words or images does the passage use to describe the problems that we face?

2

How would you summarize God's plan for dealing with these problems?

3

What do we learn about the one who would suffer on behalf of the people?

> What does this passage reveal about God's character?

> This is a very powerful and emotive passage. How does it make you feel?

* 'Transgressions' are acts that break the law.
+ 'Iniquity' means 'wrongdoing' or 'sin'.

19

PASSAGE 2

1 Peter 2:22-24; 3:18

In this extract from one of his letters, the apostle Peter is speaking about the death of Jesus Christ. He starts by quoting the Old Testament passage we just read in Isaiah.

old testament

new testament

He [Christ] committed no sin,
and no deceit was found in his mouth."*

When they hurled their insults at him, he did not retaliate; when he suffered, he made no threats. Instead, he entrusted himself to him who judges justly. "He himself bore our sins"+ in his body on the cross, so that we might die to sins and live for righteousness; "by his wounds you have been healed"...

For Christ also suffered once for sins, the righteous‡ for the unrighteous, to bring you to God. He was put to death in the body but made alive in the Spirit.

1

Did Christ deserve to die?

2

Why then did he die?

3

What was achieved by Christ's death?

According to this passage how is it possible for people who don't measure up to God's standard ("unrighteous" people) to be able to measure up to it (to be "righteous")?

Why is it important or significant that Jesus "committed no sin"?

---

* 'Christ' is an important Old Testament title applied to Jesus; it refers to the 'anointed' or chosen one who would one day rule the world.

+ 'Sins' are acts of rebellion against God.

‡ 'Righteous' means 'measuring up to a certain standard' (in this case, God's standard).

20

Pulling it together

How would you use the following diagram to summarize the key ideas of the two passages we've read?

For a brief video summary, go to matthiasmedia.com/ymb/vid4.

What is the solution to humanity's biggest problem?

John Stott wrote: "The essence of sin is man substituting himself for God, while the essence of salvation is God substituting himself for man".* What do you think about this quote?

What's your own reaction to the death of Jesus? What does it mean for your life?

Want to read more?
Mark 10:45
Romans 5:1-11
1 Timothy 2:5-6
1 John 3:1-5

★ J Stott, *The Cross of Christ*, IVP, Downers Grove, 1986, p. 160.

PASSAGE 1

Acts 2:22-24, 36

The book of Acts describes the key events that took place after the death and resurrection of Jesus, when his disciples began to spread the word about him. This passage is from a sermon (perhaps the first ever Christian sermon) preached by the apostle Peter at the feast of Pentecost in Jerusalem.

old testament

new testament

1

What were the well-known facts about Jesus' life and death?

2

What was God's involvement in Jesus dying and rising again?

3

What does the resurrection of Jesus demonstrate?

"Fellow Israelites, listen to this: Jesus of Nazareth was a man accredited by God to you by miracles, wonders and signs, which God did among you through him, as you yourselves know. This man was handed over to you by God's deliberate plan and foreknowledge; and you, with the help of wicked men, put him to death by nailing him to the cross. But God raised him from the dead, freeing him from the agony of death, because it was impossible for death to keep its hold on him"…

"Therefore let all Israel be assured of this: God has made this Jesus, whom you crucified, both Lord and Messiah."*

What do you think would have been the consequences if Jesus had stayed dead?

If Jesus has been made "Lord and Messiah", what does this mean for our world?

If Jesus has been made "Lord and Messiah", what does this mean for us personally?

★ 'Messiah' is the Hebrew form of 'Christ', which is an important Old Testament title applied to Jesus; it refers to the 'anointed' or chosen one who would one day rule the world.

PASSAGE 2

Acts 17:22-31

Later in the book of Acts, as Paul is preaching about Jesus in Athens, the local philosophers ask him to explain what this new teaching is about. He then delivers the following famous speech.

old testament

new testament

Paul then stood up in the meeting of the Areopagus* and said: "People of Athens! I see that in every way you are very religious. For as I walked around and looked carefully at your objects of worship, I even found an altar with this inscription: TO AN UNKNOWN GOD. *So you are ignorant of the very thing you worship—and this is what I am going to proclaim to you.*

In our first passage, Peter's speech was to a Jewish audienc (Acts 2). Here in our second passage, Paul is speaking to a very different audience of nor Jewish Greeks in Athens What do the two speeche have in common?

1 What is God's relationship to everyone in the world, regardless of their culture or religion?

"The God who made the world and everything in it is the Lord of heaven and earth and does not live in temples built by human hands. And he is not served by human hands, as if he needed anything. Rather, he himself gives everyone life and breath and everything else. From one man he made all the nations, that they should inhabit the whole earth; and he marked out their appointed times in history and the boundaries of their lands. God did this so that they would seek him and perhaps reach out for him and find him, though he is not far from any one of us. 'For in him we live and move and have our being.' As some of your own poets have said, 'We are his offspring.'

2 What new situation is Paul telling the Athenians about?

What hope doe Paul's speech of for humanity?

"Therefore since we are God's offspring, we should not think that the divine being is like gold or silver or stone—an image made by human design and skill. In the past God overlooked such ignorance, but now he commands all people everywhere to repent.+ For he has set a day when he will judge the world with justice by the man he has appointed.‡ He has given proof of this to everyone by raising him from the dead."

3 What does Jesus' resurrection demonstrate?

This passage is calling on all peopl everywhere to "repent". What's yo reaction to that?

---

* The Areopagus was a Council of Athens where matters of morals and religion were discussed.

+ 'Repent' means to turn around or go back; to change one's mind and behaviour.

‡ 'The man he has appointed' refers to Jesus.

Pulling it together

How would you use the following diagram to summarize the key ideas of the two passages we've read?

For a brief video summary, go to matthiasmedia.com/ymb/vid5.

Do you think it matters whether Jesus rose from the dead or not?

What does the resurrection of Jesus mean for you personally?

How do you think your life would be different if you turned back to God?

Want to read more?
1 Corinthians 15:1-8
1 Peter 1:3-5

PASSAGE 1

Matthew 6:24; 7:13-14, 24-27

The following three short texts are from the 'Sermon on the Mount', an extended section of teaching from Jesus to his disciples.

old testament

new testament

"No-one can serve two masters. Either you will hate the one and love the other, or you will be devoted to the one and despise the other. You cannot serve both God and money"…

"Enter through the narrow gate. For wide is the gate and broad is the road that leads to destruction, and many enter through it. But small is the gate and narrow the road that leads to life, and only a few find it"…

"Therefore everyone who hears these words of mine and puts them into practice is like a wise man who built his house on the rock. The rain came down, the streams rose, and the winds blew and beat against that house; yet it did not fall, because it had its foundation on the rock. But everyone who hears these words of mine and does not put them into practice is like a foolish man who built his house on sand. The rain came down, the streams rose, and the winds blew and beat against that house, and it fell with a great crash."

1

What do these three passages have in common?

2

In the third passage, how would you summarize the two responses to Jesus and his words, and the two outcomes?

What do you think it would mean to "serve" money?

What other 'masters' do people commonly serve today?

To be "narrow" is usually not a good thing in our society. Can "narrow" ever be good?

What sort of claim is Jesus making here about himself and his words?

27

PASSAGE 2

John 3:16-18, 36

This short passage from John's Gospel contains one of the most well-known verses in the Bible.

old testament

new testament

For God so loved the world that he gave his one and only Son, that whoever believes* in him shall not perish but have eternal life. For God did not send his Son into the world to condemn the world, but to save the world through him. Whoever believes in him is not condemned, but whoever does not believe stands condemned already because they have not believed in the name of God's one and only Son...

When it says that the anger of God "remains" on certain people, why would it be on them in the first place?

1

Why did God send his Son into the world?

Whoever believes in the Son has eternal life, but whoever rejects the Son will not see life, for God's wrath+ remains on them.

What's the most surprising thing in this passage, do you think?

2

What do we learn about "the world" in this passage?

How would the message of this passage fit together with other parts of the Bible we've read so far (e.g. in parts 3 and 4)?

3

How would you summarize the two possible responses to the Son of God?

What do you think it would mean to trust and rely on ('believe in') the Son?

★ To 'believe' means to trust or rely on someone or something.

✛ 'Wrath' means 'anger'.

Pulling it together

How would you use the following diagram to summarize the key ideas of the two passages we've read?

For a brief video summary, go to matthiasmedia.com/ymb/vid6.

The Bible presents us with a pretty stark choice between two ways of living—basically, God's way or our way. Which way do you want to live?

Which way do you live now?

How would living God's way change your life?

Want to read more?

Mark 8:34-38
1 Thessalonians 1:9-10

Where to from here?

We started, six sessions ago, with the challenge of reading the Bible for ourselves, and finding out its central message. But as we've done so, perhaps you've discovered what so many people have discovered over the centuries—that the more we look into the Bible, the more we sense someone in there staring back at us. We start to realize that God himself is talking to us, challenging us to recognize the truth about him and ourselves, and calling on us to turn back and to start living his way instead of ours.

The Bible presents us all with a challenge—of whether we are going to accept God's offer of forgiveness, and to live his way, with the risen Jesus as our ruler.

If you're not yet convinced about this, and you want to think and find out more, there are two easy ways to do this.

- The first is to talk to a Christian person you know (perhaps the person who has been reading the Bible with you) about a church you could go to in order to keep hearing the Bible taught and explained, and to ask your questions.

- The second is to go to www.twowaystolive.com, where you'll find not only a simple re-statement of the main message of the Bible, but also a stack of resources and suggestions for finding out more.

However, if you *are* convinced, and you know that you want to start living with Jesus as your Lord, how do you start?

The **first** thing to do is to talk to God. You need to admit before him that you have rebelled against him, that you deserve punishment, and that you're asking for mercy on the basis of Jesus' death in your place. You'll also need to ask God to help you change from being a rebel to being someone who lives with Jesus as your ruler.

You could pray something like this:

Dear God,

I know that I am not worthy to be accepted by you. I don't deserve your gift of eternal life. I am guilty of rebelling against you and ignoring you. I need forgiveness.

Thank you for sending your Son to die for me that I may be forgiven. Thank you that he rose from the dead to give me new life.

Please forgive me and change me, that I may live with Jesus as my ruler.

Amen.

The first step, then, is to pray.

The **second** step is also fairly obvious. Having prayed this sort of prayer, you will want to start putting it into practice—that is, actually submitting to Jesus. There will no doubt be all kinds of areas in your life in need of change.

You'll need to get rid of old rebellious habits (like greed, anger, selfishness, and so on) and start some new ones that please God (like generosity, kindness, love and patience).

This second step will go on for the rest of your life, but God will be with you all the way. He'll keep speaking to you (through your reading of the Bible); he'll keep listening to you and helping you (as you pray to him); he'll empower you to change and to live his way (by his Spirit who lives within you); and he'll provide brothers and sisters to encourage you along the way (as you meet with other Christians).

The second step, then, is to submit to Jesus and start living with him as your ruler.

The **third** thing you have to do is also ongoing. You need to keep putting your trust in the right place. It's only because of Jesus (and his death and resurrection) that you can be forgiven and put right with God. You'll need to keep coming back to this again and again, because as you start to live God's new way, you will still fail and do the wrong thing. We all do. We all need to keep looking back to the death of Jesus on the cross as the only grounds for our pardon. We must never stop relying on him—and him alone—as the means by which we are forgiven and granted eternal life.

And **finally**, don't think that you need to do all this on your own. One of God's great gifts to us in living his way is a fellowship of other people to encourage and help us along the way. Talk to the person who you've been reading the Bible with about how to link up with a church that can help you in your new walk with God.

Further reading

Can We Trust What the Gospels Say About Jesus?

Jesus is an amazing man; he changed human history. But can you really know anything about him? Hasn't the Bible been changed over the centuries? In this immensely readable booklet, Andrew Errington takes a careful and balanced look at some of the big questions surrounding the history of Jesus. This booklet is full of evidence, challenges and surprising conclusions. For example, did you know that the authors of the Bible were biased, and that's precisely why you should read them?

Short enough to read quickly but long enough to tackle the big questions, *Can We Trust What the Gospels Say About Jesus?* deals with the origins of the gospel stories about Jesus; how they got to us today; and evidence for Jesus from outside the Bible. If you've ever wondered what the Bible actually is, or why it's worth reading, then this is for you.

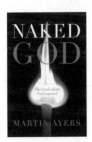

Naked God

Is there a God? And perhaps more to the point, if there is a God, what real difference will it make to my life?

These are the most basic and universal of questions, and yet we don't usually take much time to think about them. In *Naked God*, former lawyer Martin Ayers provides an opportunity for you to do just that: to ask the awkward questions, to sift through the evidence, and to get to the truth about God.

Jesus

It is no exaggeration to say that no army that ever marched, no navy that ever sailed, no government that ever sat, and no king that ever reigned has left as much of a lasting impression on the course of history as this one solitary life.

That life is the life of Jesus. But it's easy to get caught up in misinformation about who Jesus is, his history, and what he really came to do.

In this short book, Scott Petty clears away the confusion and takes us to the centre of the Bible's teaching on who Jesus is, what he came to do, and what he wants for us. Sprinkled with humour, this book will help you understand the difference Jesus makes to life, history and eternity

Just for Starters

Just for Starters provides seven simple and short Bible studies on the basics of the Christian life, looking at what the Bible teaches on seven fundamental topics:

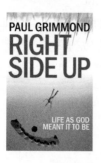

Right Side Up

This book by Paul Grimmond is especially designed for new Christians, to explain what it means to be a Christian and what the lifelong adventure of following Jesus is like. It clearly explains the message of Jesus, but also goes on to discuss the many practical issues and challenges that new believers face. It's a warm-hearted, engaging, exciting read about the Christian life.

All of these titles are available from Matthias Media—please see the next page for contact details.

Matthias Media is an independent Christian publishing company based in Sydney, Australia. To browse our online catalogue, access samples and free downloads, and find more information about our resources, visit our website:

www.matthiasmedia.com

How to buy our resources

1. Direct from us over the internet:
   – in the US: www.matthiasmedia.com
   – in Australia: www.matthiasmedia.com.au

2. Direct from us by phone: please visit our website for current phone contact information.

3. Through a range of outlets in various parts of the world. Visit **www.matthiasmedia.com/contact** for details about recommended retailers in your part of the world.

4. Trade enquiries can be addressed to:
   – in the US and Canada: sales@matthiasmedia.com
   – in Australia and the rest of the world: sales@matthiasmedia.com.au